W9-ALJ-349

STEM *trailblazer* BIOS

# IPOD AND ELECTRONICS
## VISIONARY
### TONY FADELL

ANASTASIA SUEN

Lerner Publications Company
Minneapolis

Lerner Publications Company
A division of Lerner Publishing Group, Inc.
241 First Avenue North
Minneapolis, MN 55401 U.S.A.

For reading levels and more information, look up this title at www.lernerbooks.com.

Content Consultant: Partha Dutta, Professor of Electrical, Computer, and Systems Engineering Department, Rensselaer Polytechnic Institute

Library of Congress Cataloging-in-Publication Data

Suen, Anastasia.
    iPod and electronics visionary Tony Fadell / by Anastasia Suen.
        p.    cm. — (STEM trailblazer bios)
    Includes index.
    ISBN 978-1-4677-2456-2 (lib. bdg. : alk. paper)
    ISBN 978-1-4677-2481-4 (eBook)
  1. Fadell, Tony, 1969—Juvenile literature.  2. Electronics engineers—United States—Juvenile literature.  3. iPod (Digital music player)—History—Juvenile literature.  I. Title.
    ML3930.F23S84  2014
    006.5—dc                                              232013026974

Manufactured in the United States of America
1 – PC – 12/31/13

The images in this book are used with the permission of: © David Paul Morris/Bloomberg/Getty Images, p. 4; © Gary Blakeley/Shutterstock Images, p. 5; © Wikimedia Commons, p. 7; © Susan Montgomery/Shutterstock Images, p. 8; © Hank Shiffman/Shutterstock Images, p. 9; © Blakespot/Flickr, p. 10; © Shutterstock Images, p. 12; © Lynn Goldsmith/Corbis, p. 15; © Joe Ravi/Shutterstock Images, p. 16; © Trudy Wilkerson/Shutterstock Images, p. 17; © Paul Smith/Featureflash/Shutterstock Images, p. 18; © Marcio Jose Sanchez/AP Images, p. 21; © Simon Dawson/Bloomberg/Getty Images, p. 22; © Aaron Logan/Wikimedia Commons, p. 24; © Frederic Larson/Corbis, p. 25; © Press Association/AP Images, p. 27.

Front cover: © David Paul Morris/Bloomberg via Getty Images; © Frederic Larson/San Francisco Chronicle/CORBIS (background).

Main body text set in Adrianna Regular 13/22. Typeface provided by Chank.

# CONTENTS

## Chapter 1

Tony Fadell's passion and drive helped change the world of music.

# IMPACT ON MUSIC

The year 1969 was a great one for music. Three big things happened. More than one hundred thousand people attended the four-day Woodstock Music and Art Fair in rural New York. Movie star and cowboy singer Gene Autry made the

Country Music Hall of Fame. And Tony Fadell was born. Fadell has changed the way we collect, store, and listen to music.

## LISTENING AND LEARNING

Anthony Michael Fadell was born on March 22, 1969, in Detroit, Michigan. As a child, Tony loved listening to and collecting music. He also loved **engineering**. He was curious about how things were built. Tony learned how to build and fix things at a very young age. When he was only four years old, he worked on electrical wiring projects with his grandfather.

Fadell grew up in Detroit, Michigan, a city famous for its auto engineering.

## BUILDING A PROCESSOR

When Tony was twelve, he wanted to buy an Apple IIe personal computer. But he didn't have enough money. His grandfather made him a deal. If Tony worked during the summer and put all of his earnings toward the computer, his grandfather would pay the rest. Tony worked at a golf course all summer to save up. He worked as a caddie on the course. That fall, he was able to buy his first computer.

Five years later, Tony invented a new processor for the Apple II computer. This was the part of the computer that carried out the computer's instructions. Tony got a **patent** for this invention. Apple bought the patent. As a teenager, Tony sold his idea to the company that had made his computer!

6

The first Apple computers were much larger than most modern computers.

## Chapter 2

Fadell started an educational software business with one of his professors at the University of Michigan.

# COLLEGE AND CAREER

Fadell really liked working with computers. When it came time for college, he decided to study computers at the University of Michigan. In 1991, Fadell graduated from college with a degree in computer engineering.

After college, Fadell left Michigan and went to California. He moved to an area called Silicon Valley, near Stanford University. Many Stanford engineering graduates were starting new companies there. Soon it became the place to go if you wanted to work with new technology. That was where Fadell wanted to work.

## CREATING HANDHELDS

In 1992, Fadell started working for the company General Magic. Like many other companies in Silicon Valley, it was a start-up, or new, company. The owners had worked on the Apple team that created the Macintosh computer. They wanted to make handheld communicators. These new **devices**, however, didn't quite work.

Many new tech companies started in Silicon Valley, near San Francisco, California.

The Philips Nino did not have its own keyboard like the Velo 1, but it came with a stylus pen to use on the touchscreen.

## VELO AND NINO

Fadell decided to look for another job. After working at General Magic, which was a small company, he moved to one of the biggest. He started a new job at Philips Electronics. Philips Electronics hired Fadell to be the head of its new mobile computing unit. Fadell was twenty-six years old. That made him the youngest manager in the company. Fadell's team invented two new handhelds called the Velo and the Nino. Handhelds were also called personal data assistants, or PDAs. PDAs were like small computers people could carry around in a pocket. These small devices, featuring a notepad, a calendar, contacts, and a to-do list, were becoming popular in the late 1990s.

## VELO 1

The Velo 1 was like a computer that fit in your hand. This handheld could connect to a desktop computer, but it also worked by itself. It had a small screen and its own keyboard, just like a computer. A stylus, a small pointed pen without ink, was used to press the tiny letters on the keyboard.

## Chapter 3

Fadell wanted to create a small device that could hold all the music from his CDs.

# MUSIC IN
# YOUR HAND

Fadell moved into a new job at Philips working on Internet and audio, or sound, projects. Working with audio gave Fadell a new idea. He was a big music fan. In his free time, he worked as a DJ playing music at events. He wanted to find a way to save all of his music in one small device. Then he wouldn't have to carry all of his CDs to each event.

## CREATING HIS OWN COMPANY

Fadell talked to the software company RealNetworks about creating software for small music devices. The people at RealNetworks liked the idea so much they offered him a job. Fadell accepted, but six weeks later, the company asked him to move to Seattle, Washington. The company had its headquarters there. He didn't want to leave Silicon Valley. So Fadell started his own company instead. He called it Fuse Systems, and in 1999, he hired twelve employees.

## THE PHONE CALL

On January 23, 2001, Fadell was on vacation in Vail, Colorado. He was on a ski lift when his phone rang. The people at Apple wanted Fadell to come and work for them for eight weeks. The project they wanted him for was top secret, so they wouldn't tell him what it was. They wanted him to come and find out. Fadell still owned Fuse Systems, but he liked the work Apple was doing, so he said yes.

When he went to Apple, Fadell found out they wanted him to create a small music player. This was exactly what

Fadell wanted to do! He began by studying MP3 players—new devices that could read and play MP3s, or sound files. Early MP3 players didn't hold many songs. They were also heavy and expensive. Because of this, many people still used **portable** CD players for music on the go. The people at Apple wanted Fadell to change all that. They wanted him to create a new device that held more music and was easier and more convenient to use.

## TECH TALK

"I had been doing MP3 players and handheld computers since 1990–1991, and so [Apple] sought me out because of my experience. I consulted for Apple for about eight to ten weeks, and during that time I put together the iPod concept . . . all the key pieces of the puzzle."

—*Tony Fadell*

Fadell gladly joined Apple's project to create a small music player.

## Chapter 4

Projects at the Apple headquarters in Cupertino, California, are kept very secret.

# TOP SECRET
# PROJECT

Apple's new MP3 player was top secret. Fadell and other team members weren't allowed to talk about it. Even other people at Apple didn't know about it. Fadell worked with other companies to get the parts he needed. But he couldn't

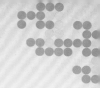

tell them what he was working on. These companies only knew what he needed them to make, nothing more.

## BUILDING A NEW MP3 PLAYER

Fadell began building new MP3 player **models** with foam boards. But the models were so light that they didn't feel real. Fadell had an idea. He went out to his garage and found the old tackle box he had used when he went fishing with his grandfather. Inside the box were some old fishing weights. He took a sledgehammer and pounded them down. Then he put the weights in one of the models. It made the model heavier. Now it felt like the real thing.

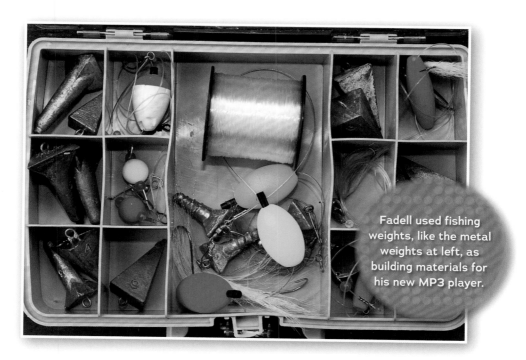

Fadell used fishing weights, like the metal weights at left, as building materials for his new MP3 player.

Fadell hoped his new MP3 player models would impress Steve Jobs (*pictured*), one of the founders of Apple.

## "DULCIMER"

Apple's secret MP3 player project was given a code name: P-68. Fadell and his team gave it a different name. They called it Dulcimer. A dulcimer is a wooden musical instrument with four strings.

In early April 2001, Fadell's time at Apple was almost up. It was time to show his bosses what he had done. They set up a meeting. Even Steve Jobs, the chief executive officer of Apple, was going to be there. Fadell had three different models to show. Before the meeting, he hid his favorite one under a wooden bowl on the table. He wanted to save it for last. When it was Fadell's turn to present his work, he showed the parts first. He showed a tiny motherboard, the main computer part that sends signals to the other parts. There was also a tiny hard drive, batteries, and a glass screen. Fadell put them on the table for everyone to see.

## SAVE THE BEST FOR LAST

The models were next. Fadell showed his first model. It had a slot at the top for a memory card. Jobs didn't like it. Fadell

## TECH TALK

"All of the other MP3 players had these little plus and minus buttons to go down a menu one song at a time. We were going to hold a thousand songs on this thing—you can't hit the plus button a thousand times! So I figured, if you can't go up, why not go around?"

—*Phil Schiller*

showed the second model. It had a cheap memory card inside, so it didn't cost much. But if the battery died, all the music had to be reloaded. Jobs didn't like that, either. Fadell lifted up the bowl and took out the finished model—the one with the fishing weights inside. It had a cover with buttons. Jobs liked it!

Phil Schiller, the vice president of marketing, showed his own models next. Some were big and some were small, but they all had a wheel on the front. Jobs asked Fadell if he could make a device with a wheel on it. Fadell said he could.

Phil Schiller has been a part of many of Apple's famous products. In 2012, he helped introduce the iPad mini.

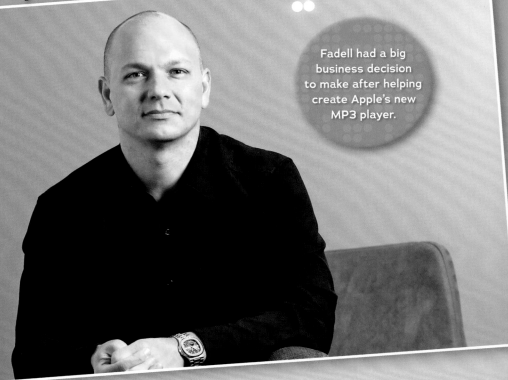

## Chapter 5

Fadell had a big business decision to make after helping create Apple's new MP3 player.

# BIG
# DECISIONS

**B**y the time Fadell presented his models, his own company had run out of money. He had a decision to make: Should he stay at Apple and fully develop this new MP3 device? Or should he make a new MP3 player at his own company?

Fadell wanted to make sure his new MP3 player would be built. He didn't want to spend time on an invention no one would be able to use. The people at Apple knew Fadell was the right man for the job. They told him that if he left, the project wouldn't be built. Fadell decided to keep working with Apple.

## BUILDING THE IPOD

Apple was ready to move forward with its exciting new MP3 device. The company didn't want to wait long to release it. Apple wanted it to come out for the next holiday season, just seven months away. Fadell began work right away. The new device was tested over and over. Fadell even took it home over the weekends to test it. Jobs met with Fadell's team every day as the deadline drew near. Before Apple put its name on the new MP3 player, it had to be just right.

### TECH TALK

"[Creating the iPod] was one foot in front of the other. . . . We were finding our way as we went. There was no grand master plan."

—Tony Fadell

The iPod's size and design impressed people right away.

## A DREAM COME TRUE

In October 2001, Apple introduced the world to the iPod. It was smaller and lighter than other MP3 players. It could fit inside a pocket, and transferring music onto it was quick and easy. People also liked being able to listen to any of their music anywhere they went. The first MP3 player had been able to hold only about eight songs. The first iPod could hold one thousand songs! Fadell's idea had become a reality.

## IPODS

Fadell kept improving the iPod. In 2004, the smaller iPod mini came out, and in 2005, the iPod shrunk two more times. Apple introduced the iPod shuffle in January and the iPod nano in September. In 2006, the iPod started doing more than just playing music. It could track your exercise too. Apple worked with Nike to create a sensor that fit in your shoe while you exercised. During the exercise, the sensor kept track of your workout. It sent information to the iPod, such as how far you had run, for you to see. Overall, Fadell worked on eighteen different iPod updates!

Steve Jobs introduced the iPod mini in 2004. It came in five different colors for buyers to choose from.

Fadell then started working on Apple's next big project: the iPhone. Just as with the first iPod, Fadell made three very different models to test. One of them even had a keyboard as part of the body. But the winning design had the keyboard built into the touch screen. People across the United States waited in line for hours outside of Apple stores in June 2007. They wanted to be among the first people to own an iPhone. Fadell also worked on the next two versions of the iPhone as its popularity continued to rise.

## STILL DESIGNING

Fadell left Apple in 2008. After spending a year in Paris, he came back to the United States. He was building a new house when an idea struck him. Why didn't someone make a new kind of thermostat? Thermostats sense the air temperature and control furnaces and air conditioners to heat or cool a building, such as your home. Some thermostats can be programmed to turn off the heat or the air conditioning at certain times. That saves energy and money. But Fadell designed a thermostat that could learn to program itself! Your movements let the Nest Learning Thermostat know when you're home. It also learns what temperature you set it to when you're around. Then it can automatically make your house the temperature that you like best.

The Nest
Learning
Thermostat has
motion sensors.

## BEING RECOGNIZED

Many people have recognized Fadell's work as an inventor. In 2012, Fadell won the first Alva Award, named after Thomas Alva Edison. This award recognizes a remarkable inventor making an impact on the world. And in 2013, *Business Insider*, a business news website, named Fadell one of the seventy-five best designers in technology.

Fadell has always studied how things were made and then tried to find a better way to build them. He knew that not everything would work the first time. It often took many tries to perfect his new ideas. His hard work has helped create the iPod, the iPhone, and the Nest thermostat. Who knows what Fadell will invent next?

# TIMELINE

**1969**

Anthony Michael Fadell is born in Detroit, Michigan, on March 22.

**1981**

Tony buys his first computer with his grandfather's help.

**1991**

Fadell graduates from the University of Michigan with a computer engineering degree.

**1992**

Fadell begins his first job at General Magic in Silicon Valley, working on handheld devices.

**1998**

The first MP3 player, the MPMan F10 from Korea, is sold.

**2001**

Fadell receives a call from Apple on January 23, asking him to work for them for eight weeks. In April, Fadell presents three new MP3 player models to Steve Jobs.

**2001**

The first iPod is sold on October 23.

**2007**

The first iPhone is sold on June 29.

**2009**

Fadell has an idea for a new invention: the Nest thermostat.

**2012**

The 250 millionth iPod is sold on January 27.

**2013**

*Business Insider* names Fadell one of the seventy-five best designers in technology.

# GLOSSARY

**devices**
pieces of equipment that do a certain job

**engineering**
designing and building

**models**
small, early examples of a future project

**patent**
a document that gives an inventor rights to make and sell a new product

**portable**
possible to carry around

# SOURCE NOTES

6   Amy Groth, "iPod Creator Tony Fadell: Here's How You Build and Ship World-Class Products," *Business Insider,* May 8, 2012, http://www.businessinsider.com/tony-fadells-advice-on-prototyping-leadership-and-innovation-2012-5.

14  Stephanie Busari, "From iPhones to Thermostats: How Tony Fadell Built Nest," *CNN,* December 5, 2012, http://www.cnn.com/2012/12/05/tech/tony-fadell-podfather-nest.

20  Steven Levy, *The Perfect Thing: How the iPod Shuffles Commerce, Culture, and Coolness,* (New York: Simon and Schuster, 2006, page 38).

23  Nilay Patel, "Inside the Nest: iPod Creator Tony Fadell Wants to Reinvent the Thermostat," *Verge,* November 14, 2011, http://www.theverge.com/2011/11/14/2559567/tony-fadell-nest-learning-thermostat.

# FURTHER INFORMATION

## BOOKS

Doeden, Matt. *Steve Jobs: Technology Innovator and Apple Genius.* Minneapolis: Lerner Publications, 2012. Find out more about the famous and visionary former CEO of Apple.

Firestone, Mary. *Wireless Technology.* Minneapolis: Lerner Publications, 2009. Learn how smartphones and other devices send and receive information without using wires.

Mullins, Matt. *Electricity.* New York: Children's Press, 2012. Get the basic science behind what powers your favorite gadgets.

## WEBSITES

### Apple iPod
http://www.apple.com/ipod
Check out all the latest iPods, large and small.

### History of the Edison Cylinder Phonograph
http://memory.loc.gov/ammem/edhtml/edcyldr.html
Follow the steps Thomas Edison took to invent the first machine that recorded sound and played it back later.

### Nest
http://nest.com
Watch a video at the Nest website to see Fadell's latest project.

# INDEX

## ABOUT THE AUTHOR

Anastasia Suen has taught everything from kindergarten to college. The prolific author of more than 160 books and the founder of STEM Friday, she writes about science, technology, engineering, and mathematics for children, teens, and adults. Suen lives with her family in Plano, Texas.